GREENING YOUR BOAT

A Successful Year-Round Plan

GREENING YOUR BOAT

A Successful Year-Round Plan

Ben van Drimmelen

Self-Counsel Press
(a division of)
International Self-Counsel Press Ltd.
USA   Canada

Self-Counsel Press acknowledges the financial support of the Government of Canada through the Canada Book Fund for our publishing activities.

Printed in Canada.

First edition: 2014

Library and Archives Canada Cataloguing in Publication

Van Drimmelen, Ben, author

    Greening your boat: a successful year-round plan / Ben van Drimmelen.

(Self-Counsel green series)

Issued in print and electronic formats.

ISBN 978-1-77040-206-5 (pbk.).—ISBN 978-1-77040-966-8 (epub).— ISBN 978-1-77040-967-5 (kindle)

    1. Boats and boating--Environmental aspects. 2. Boats and boating—Maintenance and repair--Environmental aspects. 3. Marine pollution—Prevention. 4. Water—Pollution—Prevention. I. Title. II. Series: Self-Counsel green series

TD195.B63V35 2014   363.739'4   C2014-905615-X

Self-Counsel Press
(a division of)
International Self-Counsel Press Ltd.
Bellingham, WA   North Vancouver, BC
USA   Canada

Contents

Notice to Readers

*L*aws are constantly changing. Every effort is made to keep this publication as current as possible. However, the author, the publisher, and the vendor of this book make no representations or warranties regarding the outcome or the use to which the information in this book is put and are not assuming any liability for any claims, losses, or damages arising out of the use of this book. The reader should not rely on the author or the publisher of this book for any professional advice. Please be sure that you have the most recent edition.

Preface

What gives the author the privilege and audacity to write a book on green boating? Time to provide a bit of background so it is clear who is communicating with you.

I am a west coast Canadian. Typical of that genre, I have long enjoyed playing and exploring on or in the ocean. I co-own a small but very robust sailboat (a Nonsuch, originally designed for Great Lakes sailing) and also have an inflatable Zodiac and both a single and a collapsible double kayak. I have so far made 15 eight- to ten-day kayak trips along most of the BC coast. I have also delighted in a two-week trip down the South Saskatchewan River (Alberta portion), although one persistent detraction was the extreme impact of cattle; feces and hooves plowing up the muddy shores. My sailing trips have generally been shorter, although I did spend three months exploring the waters along the northeast side of Vancouver Island and the San Juans. Other than a few days of dingy sailing in southern Saskatchewan, I have no boating experience in the vast rest of the world.

That's the boating bit. As for the environmental impacts of boating and what I know about those, I have been a wildlife biologist for about 40 years. I was also an environmental lawyer for almost 20 years.

Put it all together and I feel I am in a good position to collect information from various sources and come up with a guide to greener boating.

What triggered my specific interest in greener cruising? While kayaking, I have frequently seen rainbows of nylon ropes and netting festooned over rocks and low-hanging branches along even the most remote shores of northwestern Vancouver Island and Haida Gwaii. Just above the driftwood, a jumble of bottles, Styrofoam blocks and bits, plastic containers, lightbulbs, tangles of monofilament fishing line, more netting, ropes. Most was from fishing vessels and freighters, not recreational boaters, but the spectacle made me focus on floating garbage.

I had a more direct experience when I donned scuba gear to retrieve a friend's glasses from below a marina dock. I saw no glasses on the bottom, so I took off my gloves to explore the silt by touch. As I swam, I noticed white anemones growing from the silt, plus some small rocks on the surface. Neither should have been there. As I quickly realized my mistake — that the anemones were toilet paper and the stones were feces — I started to gag ... until I recalled that scuba regulators don't pass solids well.

Boaters freely using marinas as toilets is probably a thing of the past (although I haven't donned scuba gear to check). However, I still see boaters cleaning their vessels and discharging a bilious green cleaning fluid into marina waters. As our populations grow, the collective impacts of brown boating will inevitably grow as well. Therefore, I have written this guide so that all of us realize the potential problems and each do what we can to make changes, even small ones, that will keep our aquatic playgrounds clean and green.

I hope this book is both useful and enjoyable. Green on!

1
The Issue

*B*oating is a popular pastime. Boaters include sailors, cruisers, car toppers, canoeists, kayakers, anglers, even cruise ships; basically all of us who enjoy recreational activities on our oceans, lakes, and rivers. About 35 percent of Canadians (9.6 million people) now participate in boating, with Canadians owning some 4 million boats.[1] In the United States, there are some 75 million boaters.[2]

Boaters tend to have a strong connection with nature; a well-preserved natural environment is key to their continued participation and enjoyment. They want to protect the areas they enjoy on Canada's waterways. And they contribute very little to the problem. A European study indicated that nearly 80 percent of marine pollution comes from land-based activities, with nautical activities and especially recreational boating responsible for less than 1 percent of the overall pollution affecting the marine environment. We could therefore point accusatory fingers at industry, agriculture runoff, and storm and sanitary sewer discharge as primary causes of water pollution problems. However, our coastal and lakeside environments are very susceptible to pollution and physical damage, regardless

1 "The Economic Impact of Recreational Boating in Canada 2012," National Marine Manufacturers Association Canada, accessed August 22, 2014. www.google.ca/url?sa=t&rct=j&q=&esrc=s&source=web&cd=1&ved=0CB4QFjAA&url=http%3A%2F%2Fwww.nautismequebec.com%2Ffiles%2Ffiles%2FNMMA%2520Boating%2520Economic%2520Impact%2520Study.pdf&ei=dGDtU8iAG6SDjALK9YDoCw&usg=AFQjCNG4Ne0KVD4YdReFgm7Q0HxcvEz_pw&sig2=_Wwc1UkzyRN1CF1hHX2uAA&bvm=bv.73231344,d.cGE&cad=rja
2 "A Profile of Recreational Boating in the United States," NOAA.gov, accessed August 22, 2014. http://oceanservice.noaa.gov/websites/retiredsites/natdia_pdf/14boatus.pdf

of the sources. Rapid population growth and development are increasing pressure on the aquatic environment in many parts of Canada and the US. Public perception is also important; recreational boating tends to be misleadingly regarded as a serious source of pollution simply because of high visibility on lakes and along the coast.

Boats interact with the aquatic environment with their emissions and exhaust, propeller contact, turbulence from the propulsion systems, waves produced by movement, noise, and movement itself. Each of these interactions can have harmful effects on the aquatic ecosystem, such as sediment re-suspension, water pollution, disturbance of fish and wildlife, destruction of aquatic plants, and shoreline erosion. The full marine environment is affected:

- The air is affected by exhaust, fumes, and vapors. Exhaust residue from those old two-stroke outboard engines, for example, leaves a choking blue cloud.

- The water is impacted by disposal of our wastes and by the algal blooms that thrive on nutrients in some of those wastes. Those old outboards leave a rainbow slick. Oil, fuel, antifreeze, and other fluids collect in the bilge and are then simply pumped overboard, often by automatic pumps. Dust from sanding boat hulls and paint is toxic and settles into bottom sediment, augmented by the slow-release poisons in our bottom paints.

- The riverbanks and shoreline are eroded by the wakes and waves from our vessels, fouled by our pets during their shore leaves, and choked by oil or fuel spills or releases.

- The near-shore bottoms are scoured by turbulence (propellers lifting sediments from the bottom in shallow water, sediments which then settle on plants and reduce light penetration), propellers cutting aquatic plants, and plowing by our anchors, anchor rode and chains.

- Biological impacts include food-chain accumulation of toxins. Boating can introduce exotic plants and animals and also disperse native plants and animals into new water bodies. Water-associated wildlife is disrupted by our visual and noise disturbance, by our playful pets, by foods we leave behind or cast overboard, and by collisions with either our boats or our propellers.

These impacts gain significance because we tend to concentrate our contamination. We moor in groups in sensitive foreshore areas and in confined bays — in marinas; popular anchorages; small, protected coves, and marine parks. Weather and currents in the ocean and large lakes cannot refresh inshore waters and bays quickly, so our pollution accumulates in such areas.

So, how much of a problem is it really if a bit of trash or some fuel, oil, or cleaner goes over the side of your boat? What's the problem with a bit of sewage in the vast ocean? How bad are the toxic hull paints? Good questions.

Even if our individual impacts do not seem to be major ones, the effect of many of us in confined, protected spots adds up. Given that many of our impacts are easy to minimize, another good question arises: Why not do so?

There's a lot we can do to help ensure the health of the waters we enjoy, and this book will let you mitigate many of the environmental impacts of your boating, for cleaner, greener cruising.

2
Greening Our Fuels and Fluids: Belay That Bilge

1. What Can Get into the Water?

Gas, diesel, and oil contain some toxic hydrocarbons and heavy metals that are deadly in very low concentrations. In particular, fish and shellfish larvae are extremely sensitive to even very low levels of toxic compounds. Our refined fuels are more toxic than crude oils because they are water soluble, dispersing through the water column quickly. They are more difficult to isolate and remove once in the water and they are also more easily absorbed by an animal's soft tissues than the thick goo we see in oil spills.

Adult fish, birds, and aquatic mammals can usually leave contaminated areas, but birds and many marine mammals have natural oils that make their feathers and fur waterproof, which helps them regulate their body temperatures by trapping warm air next to the skin. Exposure to petroleum strips away the naturally insulating properties, leaving the animals susceptible to hypothermia.

Beyond immediate exposure, sustained, low-level concentrations of petroleum in calm areas like estuaries have harmful effects on bottom-dwelling organisms. Immobile fish eggs are particularly vulnerable, with fish that hatch from oiled eggs exhibiting many developmental problems. Thus, even minor fuel pollution from boats may contribute to already toxic concentrations of hydrocarbons in the water column and sediments, and increase the long-term effects on the environment.

Most boating-associated petroleum enters the water during refueling, but oil can also escape during vessel operations. One liter of spilled gasoline can contaminate 20,000 liters of water;[1] one liter of oil can cover a hectare.[2]

Discharged petroleum can also disperse through the entire water column, settling onto the bottom sediments, concentrating at the surface, or remaining suspended in the water.

2. Minimizing Fuel Spillage

One easy way to minimize fuel spillage is to not fill your boat's tank completely; fill to about 90 percent of the capacity of the tank. Heat, either from the engine or warm summer air, will expand fuel in a full tank, forcing it out of the fuel vent. Avoid overfilling by installing a fuel whistle into the fuel line above the tank. As the tank fills, the whistle sound turns into a warble and then stops completely.

Some boats tend to spray some fuel from the vent during every refueling. This can be corrected with a no-spill bottle, which fastens over the fuel vent to collect that spray. Other devices can be installed on the fuel vent line to catch the excess fuel and drain it back into the tank.

If your boat uses portable fuel tanks, you can place them on absorbent pads or trays to collect any gasoline spilled during refilling. If you do spill some fuel, don't spray detergent

---

1 "Clean Boater Handbook," Ontario Marine Operators Association, accessed August 22, 2014. www.boatingontario.ca/Portals/0/HandbookFinal.pdf
2 "Good Mate: Recreational Boating & Marina Manual," OceanConservancy.org, accessed August 22, 2014. www.oceanconservancy.org/do-your-part/green-boating/2014-good-mate-brochure.pdf

on the spill to disperse it; that detergent is more of an environmental problem than the fuel. Detergents are poisonous to all types of aquatic life if they are present in sufficient quantities, and this includes the biodegradable detergents. All detergents destroy the external mucus layers that protect the fish from bacteria and parasites and damage the sensitive gills.

3. Detergents

Detergents also have an indirect impact on aquatic life — they lower the surface tension of the water, which allows fish to more readily absorb organic chemicals such as pesticides and phenols. A detergent concentration of only two parts per million will double the amount of chemicals that fish absorb, even though that concentration is not high enough to affect fish directly.[3]

In addition to pollutants, detergents contain nutrients. Phosphates in detergents can produce algal blooms that not only deplete oxygen in the water when they decompose, but produce toxins of their own.

4. Alternative Fuels

Alternative fuel can be a good way to green your boating but there are complications. The basic problem is that boat engines tend to be old because they don't run for many hours per year and so can operate for decades. Those old engines were designed and built long before the new fuels became available. For example, the older engines were not designed for ethanol which dissolves some plastic hoses and makes rubber hoses and seals brittle, leading to dangerous fuel

---

3 "What happens when detergents get into freshwater ecosystems?," Lenntech, accessed August 22, 2014. www.lenntech.com/aquatic/detergents.htm

leaks. Another problem is that ethanol partially dissolves the gummy sludge that builds up in the fuel lines and tank as old gas oxidizes, which can get through the fuel filter and clog the carburetor. A third problem is that ethanol loves water, absorbing it until the water suddenly separates again. That water goes to the bottom of the tank, right where the fuel intake is. The water is sucked into the engine which promptly quits. Because the water is most likely to get sucked up when the boat is being rocked by waves in heavy weather, a real emergency can develop. Isobutabol can be blended with gasoline and avoids some of the problems with ethanol.

If your boat runs on diesel, biodiesel (with up to 20 percent derived from vegetable oils) is a good green option. It burns cleaner and is less toxic to marine life, though spilled biodiesel, being 80 percent petroleum diesel fuel, still has to be treated like spilled petroleum diesel or gasoline. Biodiesel will dissolve fuel line gunk and soften natural rubber seals and hoses, although not as badly as ethanol.

Propane is another alternative fuel. Propane burns 50 times cleaner than gasoline and refueling is easier and cleaner. There are no issues with water in, or long-term storage of, propane. However, propane has a significant safety issue. As it is heavier than air, it can build up to dangerous levels in the bilge where even a small spark will basically demolish your boat and, potentially, the crew.

5. Other Bilge Fluids

Boats with outboard engines usually have only water in the bilge, but bilge water on inboards will include fuel, transmission fluid, oil, antifreeze, and other fluids. Most bilge cleaners are no help to the environment since they do not alter the petroleum products; they merely break them into microscopic droplets. When those droplets are pumped out (often automatically) in the bilge water, they spread over a much larger area and affect more aquatic life. Boaters can add a manual pump shutoff switch to automatic bilge pumps to avoid automatically dumping contaminated bilge water. In addition, bilge blankets or pads soak up oil but not the water, so they are very effective at keeping your bilge, and thus the environment, clean. When the pads are saturated, you can wring out the oil for recycling and reuse the pad.

Some bilges, especially those on older diesel engines, are hard to reach and keep clean. However, even those can be handled by adding a coalescing filter to the discharge line, which prevents oil passage and absorbs an impressive amount of oil. Avoid cleaning the bilge using detergents or enzyme cleaners; recall that they are poisonous to all types of aquatic life. There are some nontoxic bilge cleaners that use microbes that digest hydrocarbons but we should avoid introducing foreign bacteria to local waters.

6. Boat Maintenance

Engines should, of course, be tuned from time to time. This not only makes breakdowns and stranding less likely, but will produce less pollution of both air and water. Oil with contaminants will corrode internal engine components if left over a lengthy storage period such as a winter lay-up, so replace the oil in the engine before storage. And recycle both the old oil and the filter, either at your marina or at a municipal waste recycling site.

Proper tuning is only part of a green engine; efficiency is another. Other than electric engines, motors have an optimal speed or rotations per minute (RPM) at which they provide maximum power. Be sure that your engine reaches its designed optimal speed by choosing a propeller with the right pitch. An adjustable-pitch propeller allows you to dial in the optimum pitch; modular propellers let you switch propellers. Make sure your propeller blades are in good condition; damaged propellers are inefficient and so waste fuel. Although that is more of an indirect environmental issue, it still has an impact.

7. Impacts of Engine Types

Then there is the effect of your engine, especially if your boat uses an outboard engine. On an older carbureted two-stroke engine, the intake and exhaust ports are wide open when the piston engages its down-stroke. That allows a good splash of mixed oil and gas to go through unburned, so that some 20 to 30 percent of the fuel is released directly into the water.[4]

No modern boater would open up a gas can and pour a couple of liters directly into the lake, but that's exactly what's happening for every ten liters of fuel used in a two-stroke motor.

Modern two-stroke engines have improved by using direct fuel injection technology. They spray mixed fuel into the cylinder, but cover the exhaust ports on the up-stroke to eliminate the escape of gas. These new two-strokes also need only half of the lubricating oil compared to the old engines.

The cleanest running conventional marine engine continues to be the four-stroke. Like your car, the intake and exhaust

---

4 "Guide to Green Boating," Georgia Strait Alliance, accessed August 22, 2014. www.georgiastrait.org/files/share/PDF/GUIDE-2010.pdf; see also "The Effects of Motorized Watercraft on Aquatic Ecosystems," Wisconsin Department of Natural Resources, Bureau of Integrated Science Services, accessed August 22, 2014. http://roundthelake.com/PIER%20WI%20DNR/lakes.pdf

valves in a four-stroke open at alternate times, so no unburned fuel will escape into the water.

The cleanest engine of all is one that runs on electric propulsion. An electric boat motor is almost silent and there are no exhaust fumes and no pollution to the air or water. These motors have few moving parts, are very reliable, and virtually maintenance-free. They have very low running costs; after a day of boating the batteries can be recharged with shore power or with renewable energy such as solar or wind energy. However, electric motors are still scarce on the water. The main concern is the limited range (six to eight hours of cruising) between charges.[5]

That may be changing, though, as solar and wind power generation become increasingly efficient. For sailboats, the propeller's turning while under sail can be used to charge batteries.

8. Winterizing Your Boat

Winterizing your boat often involves antifreeze but even so-called nontoxic or plumbing-type antifreezes are harmful in the marine environment. With care, all the water can be drained and removed from the fresh-water cooling system without requiring antifreeze. To be sure there is no water left in the cooling system, ensure that all drain plugs or valves are clear and all hoses removed and dumped. Blow air through the system to be sure all the water has been expelled.

If there is any doubt about a passage or pump, pour in just a small amount of propylene glycol antifreeze at those sites. Avoid using ethylene glycol antifreeze (blue/green color),

---

5 "Electric Propulsion Systems for Boats," Maine Electric Boats, accessed August 22, 2014. www.maineelectricboats.com/electric-propulsion

which is deadly to humans, pets, and marine organisms even in low doses. Propylene glycol (orange/pink color) is less toxic than ethylene glycol and so better suited for use in boats.[6] Even a 50:50 antifreeze/water mix will provide good freezing protection.

6 "Boating Pollution Economics & Impacts," The Regents of the University of California, accessed August 22 ,2014. http://ucanr.org/sites/coast/files/59476.pdf

3

Greening Our Paints and Cleaners: "Chore" Leave

1. Cleaning and Painting the Bottom: One Hull of a Problem

Many products used to clean both hulls and decks contain heavy metals, ammonia, phosphates, and chlorine. None of these products should be released into the water. Toxic effects on fish have generally not been observed, because fish can move away from an affected area. Of much greater concern is the indirect effect of such pollutants on fish habitat (on water quality, clarity, and on aquatic plants) which subsequently will impact fish populations. That said, filter feeders such as bivalves can accumulate high concentrations of pollutants from suspended particles.

Marine boating in particular requires periodic cleaning of your hull. Algae, slime, grass, bryozoans, hydroids, diatoms, snails, worms, barnacles, and anemones all love to live on boat bottoms and quickly attach themselves to the hull. After six months in the water, an untreated boat may burn 40 percent more fuel to overcome increased friction due to such fouling.

Most antifouling bottom paints that reduce the growth of marine organisms are toxic and poisonous; after all, they are applied specifically to repel or kill plants and animals that attach to a marine surface. In the past, such paints contained mercury, arsenic, and copper, all of which are highly toxic.

But a bottom paint is still needed that will keep those organisms off of the bottom of your boat for several years. Which bottom paint should you apply after cleaning the hull?

In essence, there are two types of bottom paint: ablative and hard bottom. If you trailer your boat or keep it on a lift, you would typically use an ablative bottom paint. Ablatives contain some poisonous biocides but they function primarily by being partially soluble so that they slough off slowly when the boat moves in the water or there is a current. It is the preferred bottom paint of most boaters since it typically lasts longer and continuously exposes a new protective outer coating as it wears.

Hard bottom paint is a modified epoxy and so is very durable. These paints dry to a porous film that is packed with biocides which leach out throughout the season as they come into contact with water. Hard bottom paint is suitable for boats that sit at dock for long periods, but it will oxidize out of the water, slowing the release of the biocides to the point where they are ineffective. Reliance on a leaching process means that hard bottom paints typically have a higher ratio of biocides than ablatives.

Unfortunately, the most common biocides are copper compounds; cuprous oxide can constitute up to 70 percent of a bottom paint's active ingredients.[1] Copper is very toxic to fish, particularly when combined with zinc sulfates; it persists in the environment and accumulates in sediments, marine plants, and animals.[2]

---

1 "Good Mate: Recreational Boating & Marina Manual," OceanConservancy.org, accessed August 22, 2014. www.oceanconservancy.org/do-your-part/green-boating/2014-good-mate-brochure.pdf
2 "Boating Pollution Economics & Impacts," The Regents of the University of California, accessed August 22, 2014. http://ucanr.org/sites/coast/files/59476.pdf

The best antifouling paints contain a boosting biocide combined with cuprous oxide, and these paints can be more environmentally friendly than other options. There is currently a great deal of research into alternative forms of biocides, particularly those of organic origin, so one cannot yet identify a most-suitable biocide. If doing your own research, brace for the long names of these substances. For example, an organic algaecide goes by the name N-cyclopropyl-N'-(1,1-dimethylethl)-6 (methylthio)-1,3,5-triazine-2,4-diamine.

There are some new coatings that are less toxic than past products. Some have a porous film with biocides in the pores which are slowly released. Still poisonous, these paints do release fewer toxic chemicals into the water than the ablative and hard bottom paints. There are also environmentally friendly bottom paints that use vinyl, Teflon, or silicon to produce slick hard hull surfaces that don't let marine organisms attach. There are no toxins in these paints, but the results tend to not last long.

Another option, probably the best environmental option at present, is a coating that leaves a layer of microfibers that move in the water, physically resisting attachment by marine organisms. A product such as SealCoat can be applied to all kinds of hulls, but it is expensive to apply, easily damaged, and cannot be repainted. These non-biocide paints work well on fiberglass, concrete, and metal boats, but are not recommended for wooden boats. They have to be applied to a very clean hull, so are best suited to new boats.

Non-biocide paint manufacturers are now developing copper sealer paints that can be applied over existing copper paints, eliminating the need to strip the old paint. They are also developing more environmentally friendly paint strippers;

biodegradable products that remove antifouling paint without toxic chemicals.

No matter which bottom paint you decide to use, bottom cleaning and repainting should only be done on dry land during the periodic haul-out where you can contain the waste products and keep them out of the marine environment. Very few shipyards have closed-loop recirculating waste systems, in part because of the cost and the difficulty of disposing the toxic sludge that is collected. Nevertheless, you can significantly reduce the problem by using dustless vacuum sanders and by using tarps or drop sheets and hull skirting to collect residue from your own cleaning, sanding, or painting. That residue can then be disposed of like any other hazardous waste.

If the bottom is already protected with antifouling paint or a bottom wax, only water is needed to clean the bottom of the boat; no soaps, detergents, or chemicals are required. If you do decide to use cleaners, the water should be discharged to a municipal sanitary sewer system or to the septic system. If your boat is trailerable, a hand-spray carwash facility likely has proper disposal methods.

A high-pressure washer will remove any algae, but it will not produce a sparkling hull without using cleaning chemicals containing acid. To avoid using these harsh chemicals, consider simply living with a slightly yellowed hull color; it won't be visible when the boat is afloat anyway.

Between haul-outs, you can simply use a soft brush or cloth to clean your hull in the water. Light rubbing, rather than scrubbing, will minimize the release of toxic bottom paint into the environment.

2. Topsides: Clearing (and Cleaning) the Decks

Many cleaning products that we use in our homes are treated at treatment plants before being discharged into local waterways. When used on boats, however, those same cleaners go directly into the water without any treatment, which can be deadly for marine organisms. Any product that recommends use in a well-ventilated area or the use of gloves to avoid skin contact will be harmful to the environment.

Cleaning products can contain biologically disruptive chemicals and poisons plus nutrients such as phosphates, ammonia, chlorine, caustic soda, surfactants, or potassium hydroxide. Many of these toxins are taken in by tiny animals which are then consumed by fish and shellfish. These toxins will bioaccumulate if they are ingested at a higher rate than they are excreted. Biologically disruptive chemicals, in particular, are persistent. They bioaccumulate and then increase concentration up the food chain, reaching the highest concentrations at the top of the ecosystem. Therefore, we need to carefully consider the selection of cleaning products we use to keep our decks and hulls bright and shiny.

One of the best, and greenest, ways to clean boat decks is simply to apply a mop or brush when the decks are wet, either from rain or dew. Drop a bucket over the side, splash a quick rinse, brush, rinse again and you're done.

Examine the boat cleaning products you have been using in the past. We all have favorite products, but it may well be time to change some products and some habits. Avoid cleaners with chemicals that are toxic, such as chlorine, formaldehyde, and ammonia. Also avoid those that emulsify; they just break the cleaning chemicals into microscopic droplets which disperse more readily into the environment.

Some greener cleaning products have organic bases such as orange, vinegar, or baking soda. New nonmetal based products are being introduced. Other cleaners are biodegradable and nontoxic. These products work just as well as traditional chemical-based cleaners.

Unfortunately, choosing environmentally friendly cleaning products can be a bit confusing. In Canada, manufacturers still don't have to substantiate claims such as "green" or "environmentally friendly." There are ecological logos on products that are made for most cleaning and maintenance chores, such as a deck traction wax that cleans nonskid boat decks and can be cleaned with plain water during the boating season; the packaging features an EcoLogo. The Canadian Environmental Choice EcoLogo indicates that a product has been certified by Environment Canada. However, that certification means only that the product has limited environmental impact, not that it is harmless. In the United States, the Green-Seal and DfE (Design for the Environment) logos are similar; "safer" does not mean safe.

Alternatively, you can use lower impact substitutes as cleaners. Many cleaning products can be made at home with a few simple ingredients. For example, vigorous rubbing can often do the same job as detergents and soaps. Hydrogen peroxide or borax can replace bleach; salt or baking soda can replace scouring.

There are also lower impact alternatives for cleaning and polishing metals. Two tablespoons of cream of tartar in a liter of hot water works on aluminum. For brass, make a paste of equal parts saltwater and vinegar, and leave on for ten minutes. Chrome cleans well with cider vinegar, and baby oil produces a fine polish. On copper, try lemon juice and salt paste. Unvarnished wood polishes well with a solution of three parts olive oil and one part vinegar. Even teak trim doesn't need harsh, acid-based chemicals for the renewal of its color and luster; natural wood oils or water-based coating do a fine job. Fiberglass stains can usually be removed with a baking soda paste. Use one part vinegar to eight parts water for windows, but dilute it more, one part vinegar to forty parts water, to clean floors.

Baking soda also has many applications in the head/toilet, sinks, shower and coolers or refrigerators — scrub with a wet cloth dipped in baking soda and, for the head, leave the soda in the head overnight with a cup of vinegar to remove most stains. To get rid of mildew, try a paste of equal parts lemon juice or vinegar and salt.

4
Greening Our Waste Disposal

1. Shrink-wrap versus Canvas

If you need to shrink-wrap your boat for winter storage, you might want to consider a reusable canvas cover for boat storage instead. If you want to continue shrink-wrapping, recycle that material. You will probably have to remove webbing and strapping materials, but also keep it clean; it may not be recyclable if it is contaminated.

2. Sewage

Whether your boat has a head with a waste holding tank or not, take advantage of shore facilities whenever you can. Shore based showers and washrooms are usually connected to municipal sewer systems or approved septic systems designed to dispose of the waste.

Black water is untreated sewage. It is definitely biodegradable, full of nutrients that can stimulate algae growth. Once those algae die off, decomposition depletes the dissolved oxygen in the water, increasing the amount of bacteria and sometimes creating dead zones where oxygen levels are so low that fish cannot survive. Such increased biological oxygen demand tends to occur in areas with many boats and little water movement.

While it is a disgusting discharge, the primary concern about sewage is its effect on water quality by exposing swimmers and shellfish to disease-causing pathogens. For swimmers, streptococci, fecal coliform, and other bacteria can cause diarrhea, dysentery, gastroenteritis, and skin rashes — and, of course, complete closure of popular areas for swimming. Filter feeders such as clams, oysters, and mussels can actually benefit indirectly because they concentrate those disease-causing organisms in raw sewage, making them unfit for human consumption — survival of the filthiest!

Any boat with toilet facilities also has to have black water holding tanks. Besides sewage, those tanks can also contain tank disinfectants, deodorants, or other chemicals that can be toxic to the marine environment. Chemical deodorizers or disinfectants kill bacteria, preventing decomposition, so the sewage just dissolves into tiny particles. Use products that are the least harmful to the environment; there are several holding tank products available that have been EcoLogo certified.

Sewage discharge is not allowed within three miles of shore or any inland water, including the Great Lakes.[1] Some jurisdictions (Ontario plus some interior lakes in British Columbia and Manitoba) also prohibit outlets that allow discharge directly into the water; Y-valves must be removed or at least sealed in a position that lets raw sewage go only into a holding tank.[2] Beyond that, discharge is allowed, being prohibited only in specifically designated water bodies such as specific narrow bays and marine park anchorages.

---

1 *Canada Shipping Act* Vessel Pollution and Dangerous Chemicals Regulations, Government of Canada, accessed August 22, 2014. http://laws-lois.justice.gc.ca/eng/regulations/SOR-2012-69/page-30.html#docCont

2 *Environmental Protection Act* Discharge of Sewage from Pleasure Boats Regulation, ServiceOntario, accessed August 22, 2014. http://www.e-laws.gov.on.ca/html/regs/english/elaws_regs_900343_e.htm

Even where there is no prohibition, you should use a shore pump-out station (available at many marinas[3]) if one is reasonably accessible. They are connected to municipal sewer systems or approved septic systems.

3. Garbage

What about that garbage? We use very durable products, so many do not decompose but get reduced to smaller and smaller particulates. Others do decompose, but do so very slowly. The worst coastal pollution offenders are plastics and Styrofoam.

It should go without saying that we should not dump any of the "top ten" offenders: cigarette butts (presumably a declining problem nowadays), food wrappers, plastic bags, plastic caps and lids, Styrofoam cups, disposable utensils, glass bottles, metal beverage cans, plastic straws/stirrers, and plastic bottles. Even if we do not dump them, the smaller items tend to blow off of, or be washed from, our decks. Keep garbage contained.

Finally, there is a Good Samaritan role that boaters can take on for waste. If you see unnatural debris, you might just want to retrieve it for proper disposal. Bring back everything you take out on a cruise, and then add one piece of garbage from someone else's wasteful wake.

3 "Ecological Green Boating Guide," The T. Buck Suzuki Foundation, accessed August 22, 2014. http://www.bucksuzuki.org/images/uploads/docs/greenboating2010_en.pdf

5
Greening Our Galleys: Altering (Food) Courses

1. Dealing with Packaging Waste

Provisioning your boat will confront you with the nuisance of waste from the packaging of items. Packaging can be a bulky imposition in limited boat space and can turn into garbage that has to be stored until it can be disposed of ashore. The easy way to minimize this problem is to repack your groceries. Remove and recycle the original packaging ashore and repack your provisions in reusable food containers; they come in diverse sizes and stack well to conserve space. Some items such as vegetables can be further prepared before departure, so you can leave peelings and inedible greens in the compost at home.

2. Sustainable Seafood

Choosing sustainable fish is a simple and effective way to help ensure that we maintain ecologically balanced lakes and oceans. Whether you are cruising, kayaking, or fishing, marine creatures offer a ready source of fresh foods.

Most of the information about sustainable fish is directed at shoppers in grocery stores, but the same information can guide you when on the water, whether you are replenishing your supplies or hunting the elusive halibut.

The SeaChoice program is operated by several Canadian environmental organizations to use science-based assessments to direct shoppers and businesses toward sustainable fisheries and aquaculture. SeaChoice produces a color-coded card with species, and countries of origin, to select for and to avoid, based on the environmental sustainability of fishing and fish farming techniques.[1]

Or, if you have a specific species in mind, you can get information on its sustainability.[2] In the US, Seafood Watch guides provide similar information on which fish is relatively abundant (OK to eat) and which species are overfished (need to avoid). They also flag types of seafood that contain levels of mercury or other persistent toxins such as polychlorinatedbiphenyls (PCBs) that pose a health risk. Seafood Watch produces guides for different areas, with the Central, West Coast, and Northeast guides most relevant to Canadian boaters.

On a broader international scale, the World Wildlife Fund has a sustainable seafood certification logo through the Marine Stewardship Council.[3] Other large organizations, such as the US Department of Commerce are working toward a similar certification mark.[4]

3. Gray Water and Dish Soaps

Gray water is any water you use for washing, showering, cleaning, and washing dishes and clothes. Even biodegradable soaps and detergents contain surfactants to create suds or foam; surfactants can plug fish gills. Dish detergents can affect the aquatic environment in many ways, particularly if

---

1 "Canada's Seafood Guide," SeaChoice, accessed August 22, 2014.
   www.reaps.org/publications/guides/seafoodguide.pdf
2 Sustainable Seafood Search, SeaChoice, accessed August 22, 2014.
   www.seachoice.org/search/
3 Marine Stewardship Council, accessed August 22, 2014. www.msc.org
4 Sustainable Seafood Certification, NOAA Fisheries, accessed August 22, 2014.
   www.fisheries.noaa.gov/op/Sustainability/Sustainable_Seafood_Certification.html

they contain antibacterial compounds such as triclosan or triclocarbon. Environmentally friendly detergents are available for dishwashing and general cleanup in the galley area, but they are still detergents which, if they have phosphate, will pollute by causing excessive algae growth. Seek out something that is phosphate-free and biodegradable but, even for those, you should be leery of products with often-baseless claims such as biodegradable, low phosphate, or environmentally friendly unless you thoroughly research the ingredients.

The best practice is simply to use as little soap as possible. You can minimize the need for soap by not letting your dishes dry; remove grease with a reusable cloth and soak those dishes before washing. If grease is abundant, such as after frying or barbecuing, you can minimize soap use by adding a thin paper plate over the regular plate, and adding the paper plates to the garbage that you will take to shore. Pre-cleaning with paper towels will have the same benefit. As for laundry and bathing, most of that can be done ashore; even on extended cruises, most of us want the amenities of a marina now and then.

4. Kitchen Scraps

I am somewhat conflicted on what to do with compostable kitchen scraps. They soon reek if stored aboard but, more to the point, there are all kinds of crabs, prawns, shrimp, and other crustaceans waiting below to enjoy my surplus vegetable material and meat scraps. Still, it is undeniably unappealing to pass through a line of floating kitchen scraps such as banana, orange, grapefruit, and carrot peels, onion skins, and lettuce leaves that someone has chucked overboard. Make your own call on how to deal with your compostables.

6
Greening Our Operations

1. Erosion: Taking Wake Control

Some boats leave impressive wakes, bouncing moored boats and docks and spooking boaters in small sailboats, canoes, and kayaks. Slowing down is a courtesy matter, although in many places you can be fined for careless operation if your wash adversely affects the shoreline or wetlands.[1] Shoreline erosion along normally protected areas can be a major source of water pollution, damaging inshore fish habitat.

In some locations like marinas, speed limit signs are posted. In Ontario, Manitoba, Saskatchewan, Alberta, and the inland waters of British Columbia and Nova Scotia there are also unposted speed limits of 10 km/h within 30 meters from shore.[2] These limits control speed but not necessarily wakes, so every boat owner should be fully aware of the vessel's wake and travel at low-wake speeds within a half mile of potentially erodible shores.

A similar issue can arise when operating motorized dinghies, smaller outboards, or personal watercraft in shallow water or close to estuaries and wetlands. These are sensitive fish and wildlife habitats that are easily disrupted by waves

---

1 Small Vessel Regulations, Government of Canada, accessed August 22, 2014.
   http://laws-lois.justice.gc.ca/eng/regulations/SOR-2010-91/
2 Vessel Operation Restrictions Regulations, Government of Canada, accessed August 22,
   2014. http://laws-lois.justice.gc.ca/eng/regulations/sor-2008-120/

from wakes and should be navigated very slowly or, if possible, avoided entirely.

Compared to the effects of wind and the effects of land-based discharges, most recreational boating does not affect water clarity. However, boats in shallow lakes, shallow parts of lakes and rivers, and channels connecting lakes can affect water clarity by lifting and re-suspending fine bottom sediments. This temporarily reduces visibility, which affects the ability of fish to find food, the depth to which aquatic plants can grow, dissolved oxygen content, and water temperature. Those sediments then settle and smother aquatic vegetation and shellfish. Serious sedimentation is restricted to depths less than two meters but varies with boat size, engine size, speed, and the nature of the bottom such as sediment particle size.[3]

Shallow water running can also do physical damage, eroding or collapsing embankments. Propellers can cut into seagrass beds, trenching the bottom and uprooting vegetation and roots. This is particularly true of personal watercraft that use powerful water jet propulsion systems.

2. Anchoring: Oh Buoy

Relatively shallow, sheltered bays are choice sites for moorage and anchoring. Those same sheltered bays often support aquatic vegetation such as eelgrasses in dense, extensive beds or meadows. These aquatic meadows are an important component of coastal ecology, providing food, shelter, and protection for many juvenile fish and shellfish and food for waterfowl. They provide important corridors of protection and food for migrating fish. In addition, the meadows stabilize the substrate, thus reducing coastal erosion.

---

3 "The Effects of Motorized Watercraft on Aquatic Ecosystems," Asplund, T. R., 2000, accessed August 22, 2014. http://roundthelake.com/PIER%20WI%20DNR/lakes.pdf

A metal anchor and dragging chain in such sensitive habitat will grind at aquatic vegetation. A dragging anchor can plow the bottom, uprooting and destroying important plants that serve as food and cover for thousands of aquatic species.

Damage from scouring by anchors and both anchor chains and rode is particularly obvious in vegetated bottoms; gaps are left when swaths of plants are torn up.

Underwater damage caused by a single anchor or propeller may seem rather small — a little furrow along the bottom. However, the combined effect of these scrapes and gouges can be quite dramatic over a summer boating season. If mooring buoys are available, use them; their fixed foundations do less harm than dispersed anchors. If you do anchor, try to avoid vegetative beds. Eelgrasses need sunlight, so you are less likely to plow up the beds if you anchor in water deeper than four meters.

3. Waterways

There are boating impacts on the ecology along and in our waterways. Canada's quarter million kilometers of coastline is home to more than 10,000 marine-associated species. And that isn't counting the freshwater species that live in and along our lakes and rivers; the Great Lakes alone have a total shoreline of 16,000 kilometers. The general effects of pleasure boating on fish and wildlife species are not well known. Vessel movements and noise are not likely to disturb fish significantly, but pleasure boating can alter fish habitats by increasing turbidity, damaging aquatic plants, and creating turbulence, all of which presumably will harm fish at various life stages. Aquatic birds are clearly affected, as indicated by increased predation on the young and reduced breeding success. Marine mammals respond to boats with avoidance, or flight behavior, such as moving from resting sites and increasing the time and frequency of diving. While specific impacts may be hard to demonstrate, it is clear that boaters interact with, and affect, coastal ecologies, so minimizing boating impacts on particularly complex or sensitive ecological associations is important.

4. Avoiding Sensitive Spots: Standing Off

Estuaries are special transition areas between land and sea, where fresh water from rivers, creeks, or streams mixes with saltwater from the sea. They occur in bays, lagoons, harbors, inlets, marshes, sloughs, sounds, or swamps. These unique ecosystems, affected by both fresh and saltwaters and sheltered from winds and waves, have many important environmental values. This stable environment allows for the proliferation of fringe marsh and submerged aquatic vegetation.

These plant communities provide habitat and food for all kinds of birds, mammals, fish, and insects. They are nurseries for many marine organisms, including many of our favorite fish and shellfish species. Estuaries often include wetlands that filter water from the rivers and streams, intercepting and holding sediments and pollutants. Boaters should therefore minimize both physical impacts (damage to the intertidal and to the near shore) and disturbance impacts in estuaries.

Lake ecosystems vary enormously, depending on their size, depth, and location. Lakes have traditionally been considered closed, balanced ecosystems with water and nutrients constantly being recycled. However, a lake's enclosed nature also makes it highly vulnerable to pollution and to nutrient-generating activities. Lakes also support inlet and outlet marshes that can be nearly as productive as their coastal cousins.

Mussels, clams, and oysters are an important food resource on the coast, but there are myriad other shellfish and crustaceans that have environmental value. The filter feeding shellfish are very sensitive to pollution. Young oysters, when they reach the stage of seeking anchorage, are particularly sensitive to boat wakes, so if you see that the intertidal zone has oyster beds, minimize your wake.

Another special coastal habitat, one particularly sensitive to boating, is eelgrass beds. Eelgrass roots grow horizontally and are the main means of the plant's propagation. Such growth creates dense, extensive beds or meadows, creating a productive and diverse habitat. Eelgrass beds are thus an important component of coastal ecology, containing a dense and strikingly rich assemblage of vertebrates and invertebrates, providing food, shelter, and protection for many juvenile fish and shellfish and food for waterfowl. In addition, the meadows stabilize the subtidal substrate, thus reducing coastal erosion.

5. Wildlife Considerations

Boat activity causes many wildlife species to be disturbed from a variety of activities such as nesting, resting, and feeding. For some species, this is just a temporary nuisance but for other species, high frequency boat activity can have effects on the entire population. Concentrated wildlife areas are an example. Stay more than 100 meters away from bird nesting colonies so that the adults don't have to leave the eggs and young vulnerable to predators. Most marine birds do not nest in colonies; they nest on the ground or in burrows on small islets, cliffs, and shorelines. These nests are more difficult to see than noisy nesting colonies, but if you find yourself strolling in an apparent nesting area, make a gentle retreat. Many shorebirds are also particularly vulnerable because they have few choices in resting and feeding locations during their lengthy spring and late summer migrations. Letting your dog frolic along a mud flat or sand beach will cause these birds to burn up essential calories that they require for travel.

It has proven to be difficult to assess the impact of boating (compared to other disturbances) on various species of marine mammals. Non-powered craft such as sailboats seem to have less overall impact than powered craft, with speed boats and personal watercraft most likely to cause adverse behavior. However, less impact does not mean no impact, so boaters should watch marine mammals closely and try to stay far enough away to not alter their behavior in any detectable way.

Do not chase whales and porpoises; approach them from the side, not from in front or behind. Let them know your location if you don't have an engine running; tap the side of the boat with your hand from time to time. Keep more than 100 meters away (greater distances from endangered orca whales are enforced in northwestern Washington State waters) and limit your observation time to half an hour.[4] Sea lions and seals leave the water to rest between periods of foraging activity, and they can be even more sensitive to disturbance at such haul-outs, so keep at least 200 meters away.

The signs of disturbance can be subtle. With whales, dolphins, and porpoises, you will see sudden changes in direction or speed. Seals and sea lions will increase their movement toward water and increase their vocalizations, although sometimes the first sign of disturbance is just several animals raising their heads simultaneously. Seals and sea lions in some more remote coastal locations are spooked unusually easily, so

---

4 "Marine Mammal Viewing Guidelines and Regulations," NOAA Fisheries, accessed August 22, 2014. http://alaskafisheries.noaa.gov/protectedresources/mmv/guide.htm

increase your distance if the animals appear to be paying you more attention and becoming restless.[5]

6. Ecological Reserves

In BC, ecological reserves were selected to preserve and protect special natural ecosystems. These biological gems safeguard plant and animal species, features, and phenomena. Many are on attractive west coast islands. Some are closed to the public due to the sensitivity of sea bird and sea mammal colonies, but most accommodate non-destructive activities such as nature appreciation, wildlife viewing, bird watching, and photography. Ecoreserves have little signage or supervision. Basically, ecoreserves are subject to "faith-based management"; the provincial government just hopes visitors will co-operate in caring for these areas. That leaves it up to boaters to locate, and be gentle with, ecological reserves.

7. Exotic Species: There Be Stowaways

The introduction and spread of exotic species into any ecosystem is almost always undesirable. With no natural predators, such species can eliminate native species by altering their habitat, feeding on them excessively, or by using up food sources of native species. Zebra mussels and Eurasian milfoil are aggressive invader species easily transported to a new lake or stream. In Ontario, add Eurasian ruffe and spiny water fleas to the list of problem exotics.

The zebra mussel was introduced to Lake St. Clair in the early 1980s and quickly expanded its range throughout the Great Lakes. By firmly attaching to any solid surface, including hulls of boats, rigging, and motors, they have caused

---

5 The cause of this increased caution is unknown, but may be a reaction to an old-time practice of crews on fishing vessels shooting at animals that compete with them for fish.

tremendous problems by blocking industrial water intakes. To be fair, they also can have some beneficial environmental effect: They filter microscopic particles such as algae from the water, increasing water clarity and reducing pollution. Unfortunately, simply by allowing more sunlight to penetrate the water column, the zebra mussel can disrupt habitats of native fish and other organisms.

Eurasian water-milfoil was first discovered in Canada in Lake Erie in 1961. It has spread into many inland lakes throughout southern and central Ontario and Quebec, including all the Great Lakes and the St. Lawrence River. It also occurs in British Columbia and has been reported in Manitoba. Again, the environmental effects are mixed. It clogs surface waters, impeding boating. However, it also provides additional habitat and shelter in the water column for many aquatic organisms, enriching the diversity of entire food chains.

By now, most inland boaters are aware of the problems that can arise from the establishment of, and control efforts for, invasive exotics in many of Canada's lakes and rivers. Boaters can easily spread these organisms on or in trailerable boats. Before moving between lakes or rivers, pump and flush the bilge and any live well tanks on shore. Rinse boats and trailers thoroughly.

7

Greening Our Marinas: It's "Aboat" Time

*M*arinas are central to most boating, but they are also a potential source for some of the most damaging types of water pollution. Commercial marinas can discharge sewage, food waste, fish cleanings, bilge and ballast water releases, and other materials associated with boat and shipyard maintenance.

Boat maintenance can release new paint, old paint scrapings, antifoulants, solvents, oil and grease, fuels, and cleaning agents into surrounding waters. Boat traffic and dredging in marinas and in shallow navigation channels can churn up sediments, reintroducing metals, nutrients, organic matter, and toxins into the water. Although some metals can be broken down by microorganisms, most will accumulate in sediments, marine plants, and animals, and therefore persist in the environment. Creosoted pilings have aromatic hydrocarbons that may produce significant pollution in confined dock areas.

Marina owners are uniquely situated to minimize pollution created by their facilities. Boaters can help by encouraging their marina owners to get green-certified or by supporting marinas that are environmentally conscious. In Ontario, there is a Green Marine Program. Marinas can go through a third-party environmental audit against standards in a "Clean Marine Operations Handbook," which includes more than 200 specific practices. The Ontario program and its comprehensive handbook were adapted for BC in 2008 as a Green Marine BC program. Marinas can go through a similar independent audit to determine their level of environmental responsibility and receive an "eco-rating." A list of BC eco-rated marinas, plus marinas in the process of certification, is maintained by the Georgia Strait Alliance (georgiastraight.org). Boating Ontario provides a similar listing for that province.[1]

There are a number of practices and rules that marinas can implement to minimize environmental harm:

- Cleaning of hulls in the water, either by divers or underwater scrubbing devices, should be eliminated. Thus, a green marina should require that boat hulls with soft or ablative antifouling paint not be scrubbed or cleaned in the marina itself; haul-out facilities should be used for these coatings.

- Marinas should prohibit the use of mechanical devices or scrapers that remove paint underwater.

- Divers should not be allowed to leave any sort of material in the marina water, including film, debris, or metals such as zinc.

- Marinas should ban all discharge of oil, fuel, or antifreeze into marina waters; they should have absorbent pads available for boaters to soak up oil and fuel in bilges.

- Marinas should encourage boaters not to discharge contaminated bilge water into marina waters. Marinas can do this by asking boaters to add a manual pump

---

1 Boating Ontario, accessed August 22, 2014. www.boatingontario.ca/CleanMarine/ EcoRatedMarinas.aspx

shutoff switch to automatic bilge pumps to avoid periodically dumping bilge water while berthed.

- Boaters should be advised to ensure that oil, antifreeze, or other such liquids are not allowed to drain into the bilge; instead, they should be advised to use pumps to drain engine oil directly into containers so that waste oil and antifreeze can be recycled onshore.

- Marinas should remind boaters that they should not use detergents or soaps on fuel, oil, or otherwise contaminated bilge water. (While enzyme-based bilge cleaners are generally safe to use, it may take some time before the oil sheen is gone. It is best to remove contaminated water and dispose of it onshore.)

- At the fuel dock, boaters should be encouraged not to top-off or overfill tanks and to place a bucket or an absorbent pad at the fuel vent in case of accidental overflow. Absorbent pads should be available at the dock so that boaters and fuel dock attendants are not tempted to hose down accidental fuel spills or use detergents or soaps to clean up spills.

- Ideally, each marina should have a pump-out station or pump-out service but, if not, boaters should be informed of nearby pump-out locations and encouraged to use such facilities.

- The marina should encourage boaters to rinse their boats periodically to reduce the need to scrub the top-side with harsh cleaners. The marina should advise boaters that, if cleaners are used, they must not produce visible suds or discoloration of the water.

- Boaters should be allowed to do only minor touch-up painting of boats that are in the water, with any paint mixing restricted to being done onshore, not on the dock or the deck of the vessel. Any major painting or refinishing should be done on land at a boatyard, using tarps to capture all dust, drips, and debris.

- No pressure washing should be allowed, even in up-land areas, except on approved pressure wash pads.

- Spray painting, if allowed at all, should only be allowed in contained, screened areas on land at a boatyard.

- Many marinas will collect and recycle oil, antifreeze, aluminum, and plastic bottles. In addition, most offer toilets, laundry, and shower facilities. These services mean that boaters can have much less waste to deal with, and that the waste will be properly disposed of.

8

Greening the Uplands: Shore-Based Issues

*T*o this point, we have focused on greening the direct impacts of our own boating. However, there is value in broadening that focus. According to Greenpeace International's "Plastic Debris in the World's Oceans" (2006), more than 80 percent of marine pollution is land-based, so our concern about protecting the aquatic and nearshore environments that we enjoy includes doing what we can to protect them from other shore-based impacts.

The big problem in trying to protect our waters from shore-based damage is that most pollutants are delivered into the waterways from many minor points. Individually, each pollution source is small and insignificant, but their cumulative impact is immense. While the big oil spills get media attention, at least a third of the oil pollution in our waters comes out of drains as waste and as runoff from our cities and industries. Fertilizers from farms and lawns along many of our rivers and lakes trickle into those waterbodies. Plastic bags and containers, ropes and netting, packing materials, and glass bottles are thrown or washed overboard from hundreds of vessels, hundreds of kilometers away. From most small communities, and even from some big cities like Victoria, untreated or under-treated sewage seeps or flows into rivers, lakes, and the ocean. What are green boaters to do?

We cannot do much directly. The problem is national, international, even global in scope, so solutions must be implemented at those lofty levels. However, concerns can be raised with government through our members of Parliament and our members of our Legislative Assemblies.

In addition, green boaters can join or support national and international nongovernment organizations that are encouraging governments and the public to control pollution sources, such as the World Wildlife Fund's Global Marine Program,[1] the US Natural Resources Defense Council,[2] or Pollution Probe.[3]

If your interest is closer to home, there are provincial and regional organizations such as the Georgia Strait Alliance[4] and the Lake of the Woods District Property Owners Association.[5] In the US, an example from the northeast is Citizens Campaign for the Environment. There is also the Canadian Environmental Network, a collection of provincial affiliates, which can direct you to nonprofit, nongovernmental environmental organizations across Canada.[6]

If you prefer to support a local organization, you will have to make local inquiries. Some provinces have a convenient listing of environmental nongovernment organizations; the Ontario Environmental Network's Environmental Directory,[7/8] searchable by community, is an example. Internationally, there is an affiliation of some 200 local "waterkeeper" groups that

1 "Safeguarding our oceans and coasts," WWF Global, accessed August 22, 2014. http://wwf.panda.org/what_we_do/how_we_work/conservation/marine
2 "Water," Natural Resources Defense Council, accessed August 22, 2014. www.nrdc.org/water/default.asp
3 "New Approach to Water Management," Pollution Probe, accessed August 22, 2014. www.pollutionprobe.org/whatwedo/water.html
4 Georgia Strait Alliance, accessed August 22, 2014. www.georgiastrait.org
5 "Living Green at the Lake," Lake of the Woods District Property Owners Association, accessed August 22, 2014. http://lowdpoa.com/wp-content/uploads/Living-Green-at-the-Lake-Guide-website-file.pdf
6 Citizens Campaign for the Environment, accessed August 22, 2014. www.citizenscampaign.org/about.asp
7 Canadian Environmental Network, accessed August 22, 2014. http://rcen.ca/about
8 Ontario Environment Network, accessed August 22, 2014. www.oen.ca/dir

patrol rivers, lakes, and coastal waterways. For Canadian organizations, go to Waterkeepers Canada.[9] For American organizations, check the Waterkeeper Alliance.[10]

Many of these nongovernment organizations, especially the smaller ones, are volunteer-based and poorly resourced, so they tend to evolve and change over time. Accordingly, their websites come and go. Therefore, you will have to do a bit of your own searching to find one that matches your green boating interests.

9 "Your Local Waterkeeper," Waterkeepers Canada, accessed August 22, 2014. www.waterkeepers.ca/local.html
10 "Find Your Waterkeeper," Waterkeeper Alliance, accessed August 22, 2014. http://waterkeeper.org/local-waterkeepers/find-your-waterkeeper

9
Greening Our
Neighbors:
Leading by Example

*B*eyond being a green boater yourself and helping your marina to do its bit, you can have a greening influence on your boating neighbors. No need to be a zealot, but you can have a strong influence just by discussing boating impacts on the environment. Raise the topic with boaters in adjacent slips, at the pubs and restaurants at marinas. Boaters prefer some privacy at popular anchorages, but there are occasions to interact at docks and park facilities. Boaters are generally eager to become informed stewards of the amenities they enjoy.

If you have the time (such as being happily retired), you can even get into advocacy — find a problem and lobby to fix it. As a small example, I noticed a paradox when I sailed into our local marine parks. I could anchor for free, but there was a $10 fee to use mooring buoys. I anchored, but when I raised the anchor, I found it wrapped with eelgrass. So, the paradox: If parks management was serious about protecting the marine environment, boaters should be encouraged to use the buoys rather than rip up the bottom with anchors. Instead, anchoring was free and there was a financial penalty for doing the right thing for the environment. The incentive was backward.

I did some research. I found that most of our 25 local marine parks have eelgrass beds in their popular anchorages;

however, only six have mooring buoys to ease anchoring pressure. Although the parks managers had made some efforts to educate boaters with signs, it was not enough. There is a need for change in the mooring buoy/anchoring policies in nearby provincial and national marine parks. I wrote a short report that included recommendations to provide signage and brochures to inform boaters about the location and sensitivity of local eelgrass beds and best anchoring practices. I recommended that parks should install and maintain mooring buoys in all marine park areas that have popular recreational boat anchorages and eelgrass beds. And I recommended that parks should not charge a fee to use mooring buoys, but instead should charge a fee for boaters who choose to anchor in, and thereby damage, eelgrass beds. At this time, I continue to go to meetings and nudge government; the outcome is still uncertain. But it is an example of how you, as a green boater, can take direct action to try to resolve a perceived problem.

I have also taken simpler direct action with the marina where I keep my vessel. I inquired, as a client, about how it was doing in getting Green Boating certification. The response was bureaucratically vague: "Management is aware of such initiatives, and is intending on joining one and becoming certified ... Research is being done and a recommendation put forward at which time a decision will be made and communicated to the boaters/tenants appropriately." Not good enough. There were long delays in responding to my follow-up emails, but I persisted; it takes very little time to send a nagging email. After six months of delay, I threatened to visit the office for a face-to-face meeting, and that finally produced a substantive reply. The marina has now paid to enroll in the program and is considering the changes required to achieve certification. A small and partial victory, but a victory nonetheless.

Another excellent avenue to make a green impact is to volunteer in shore and marina cleanup programs, particularly in areas that are only accessible by boat. There is a national shore cleanup day scheduled twice per year, with participation in every Canadian province.[1] Internationally, Ocean Conservancy in the United States reported that 650,000 volunteers in some 90 countries picked up more than 5,000 metric tons of shoreline trash in 2013 alone.[2]

1 "Facts & Figures," Great Canadian Shoreline Cleanup, accessed August 22, 2014. www.shorelinecleanup.ca/en/content/facts-figures
2 "International Coastal Cleanup," Ocean Conservancy, accessed August 22, 2014. www.oceanconservancy.org/our-work/international-coastal-cleanup

10
Greening the End: Derelict Disposal

*M*odern composite boats are very durable, so most boat owners will not have to deal with environmentally friendly disposal of a vessel; usually, one's boat can be sold.

The problem arises when a boat gets so old and run down that the costs of repair and maintenance exceed the value of the boat. The age of a large portion of registered vessels is now 30 years or more, which is about the average lifespan of a recreational craft.[1] Therefore, as time goes by, we are going to have to deal with an increasing number of older vessels.[2] More and more boat owners are ready to discard such vessels, but those modern materials can be difficult to recycle. (Sadly, the disposal task is aggravated in Canada and other places because, unlike jurisdictions such as Washington State,[3] Canada currently has no derelict vessel removal program that contributes to the cost of removal.) The result is that an old, tired vessel is frequently abandoned or beached, leaving waves, tides, and storms to slowly demolish the wreck. In the short term, neglected or unmaintained vessels are likely to sink and release fuel, oil, sewage, and toxic chemicals into the water. Longer term, bits of the boat, along with clothing, bedding,

---

1 "EU Affairs: Environment," European Boating Industry, accessed August 22, 2014. www.europeanboatingindustry.eu/eu-affairs/environment
2 "Study of the extent of abandoned and derelict vessels in Canada," Transport Canada, accessed August 22, 2014. www.islandstrust.bc.ca/poi/pdf/derelictvesselreport.pdf
3 Washington State's derelict vessel removal program is funded by a surcharge on vessel registration fees. The program can cover up to 90 percent of the cost of removal and disposal.

paint, batteries, electronics, and other pollutants, are left to litter the beach, often for decades. That is neither effective nor environmentally responsible.

Removal and disposal of an abandoned boat are the responsibility of the boat owner, but the ownership of such derelict vessels is often difficult or impossible to determine. Even if a green boater doesn't need to dispose of his or her own vessel, an understanding of the process of disposal can help boaters to organize a community-based removal.[4]

The first, and absolutely essential, step is getting legal possession of the abandoned boat. Placing a line on an abandoned vessel does not give the finder ownership of a vessel; neither does the myth of "finders, keepers." If the owner is unknown or uncooperative, in Canada you will need Transport Canada's Receiver of Wrecks to officially declare the boat a wreck and authorize a person or community organization to take possession.[5] In the US, states have their own similar process. Typically, a state agency acts through some authorized public entity, which must first get custody of a vessel and then obtain various permits and authorizations to ensure that the disposal is done cleanly.[6]

The next step is removal of any contaminants: Fuel and oil tanks need to be checked and any petroleum products should be pumped into barrels and disposed ashore. Salvageable equipment attached to the vessel (e.g., aluminum rigging, anchor equipment) can be sold. Removable waste material should be transferred to a skiff or barge alongside and then taken

---

4 "Best Practices for the Responsible Disposal of Derelict Vessels," Living Oceans, accessed August 22, 2014. www.livingoceans.org/sites/default/files/Derelict-Vessel-Disposal-Best-Practices.pdf
5 Marine Safety and Security, Transport Canada, accessed August 22, 2014. www.tc.gc.ca/eng/marinesafety/service-standards-menu.htm
6 For an example, see: "Derelict Vessel Removal Program Guidelines," Washington State Department of Natural Resources, accessed August 22, 2014. www.dnr.wa.gov/Publications/aqr_dv_guidelines_0907.pdf

ashore and sorted for recycling or disposal — wood, plastic, metal, electronics, glass, plus hazardous materials such as batteries, paint, asbestos, and petroleum products. Once removable items and potential contaminants have been taken off, the hulk can safely be beached, which will simplify removal. It may be worth cutting some holes in the hull so that it will not start floating again in a high tide or winter storm, before removal can be completed.

The hulk probably will have to be partially dismantled on the shore. Put a boom around it to contain any debris loosened during the dismantling. Remove whatever you can (e.g., the cabin, foredeck, railings, hatch covers). Drag the remaining hull further on shore so it can be cut into transportable pieces, sorting out recyclable materials such as the engine, fuel tanks, propellers and shafts. Whatever is left will have to go to a landfill because there is still no way to recycle many of the composite materials used in modern vessels.

At the end, all that should remain is the warm feeling that a local hazard has been safely and soundly removed, recycled, and disposed of.

Appendix I:
Organizations That
Can Help You

*Y*ou will have questions and issues that are not covered in this book. In addition, you may want more detail on issues that are covered. And some of you will be in the USA or elsewhere; this book is directed at Canadian boaters first because I am most familiar with Canadian waters and issues.

The Internet allows easy location of helpful information on almost any topic, so a long list of organizations that can provide information or assistance is not necessary. In addition, websites change and evolve, so a list could soon become obsolete. Therefore, you should do your own up-to-date searching. However, to get you started, here is a short list of sources that I have found useful in the past.

Coast/Shore Debris Collection

Great Canadian Shoreline Cleanup:

www.shorelinecleanup.ca/search/cleanups

Ocean Conservancy:

www.oceanconservancy.org/our-work/marine-debris

Derelict Vessels

Transport Canada's Receiver of Wrecks:

www.tc.gc.ca/eng/quebec/marine-wrecks.htm

United States Coast Guard:

www.uscg.mil/proceedings/spring2011/articles/28_
Bright.pdf

Financial Assistance

Boating BC Association's support for nonprofit organizations for boating-related environmental stewardship:

www.boatingbc.ca/about/grant-program

American grants funding website for nonprofit grants, grant assistance programs, state grants, city grants and local grants:

www.grantwatch.com

Laws and Regulations

Canada Shipping Act, 2001; Competency of Operators of Pleasure Craft Regulations; Small Vessel Regulations; Collision Regulations; Vessel Operation Restriction Regulations; and Vessel Pollution and Dangerous Chemicals Regulations:

www.tc.gc.ca/eng/acts-regulations/acts-2001c26.htm

Transport Canada's "Safe Boating Guide." See particularly pages 52-54:

http://www.tc.gc.ca/media/documents/marinesafety/
TP-511e.pdf

US Coast Guard's compilation of federal and state boating laws:

http://www.uscgboating.org/regulations/

Marina Environmental Recognition

Georgia Strait Alliance's environmental recognition program for BC marinas, yacht clubs, and boatyards:

www.georgiastrait.org/node/425

Boating Ontario's environmental recognition program for Ontario marinas, marine dealerships, and yacht clubs. Also lists businesses that will recycle shrink-wrap:

www.boatingontario.ca/industry/Home.aspx

Michigan Clean Marina:

www.miseagrant.umich.edu/michigan-clean-marina-program

Virginia's Clean Marina Program's list of 20 American state clean marina programs:

http://web.vims.edu/adv/cleanmarina/stateprograms.htm

Recycling Information

Disposal of household hazardous and special waste:

www.productcare.org

Earth911, which features a list of recycling centers in the USA, searchable by waste category and city:

http://search.earth911.com

Kawartha Marine Boat Wrecking & Recyclers (Ontario):

http://kawarthaboatwrecking.com

Used Oil Management Association:

www.usedoilrecycling.com

Recycling Council of BC, 1-800-667-4321:

www.rcbc.ca/services/recycling-hotline

Resource Recovery Fund Board (Nova Scotia):

putwasteinitsplace.ca

Reporting Pollution

BC and Yukon:

1-800-889-8852

Alberta, Saskatchewan, Manitoba, Ontario, and Northwest Territories:

Arctic:

1-800-265-0237

Quebec:

1-800-363-4735

Maritimes:

1-800-565-1633

Newfoundland and Labrador:

1-800-563-9089

US Environmental Protection Agency, Pacific Northwest:

1-800-424-4372

US Environmental Protection Agency, New England:

1-888-372-7341

US Environmental Protection Agency, Upper Midwest:

1-312-353-2000

US Environmental Protection Agency, Midwest:

1-800-223-0425

Sewage Pump-outs

T. Buck Suzuki Foundation, pump-out station locations in BC, Quebec, and Maritimes:

www.bucksuzuki.org/images/uploads/docs/greenboat-ing2010_en.pdf

Bluenose Coastal Action Foundation, pumpout station locations in Nova Scotia, New Brunswick, and Prince Edward Island:

www.coastalaction.org/downloads/CB/cleanboat_guide.pdf

Washington State Parks, pump-out locations in Washington:

www.parks.wa.gov/657/Pumpout

Rhode Island Department of Environment Management, includes pump-out locations in Connecticut, Maine, Massachusetts, New Hampshire, and New York as well as Rhode Island:

www.dem.ri.gov/programs/benviron/water/shellfsh/pump

North Carolina Department of Environment and Natural Resources, pump-out locations in North Carolina:

http://portal.ncdenr.org/web/cm/find-pump-out-stations

NJBoating.org, map showing pump-out locations in New Jersey:

http://crssa-ext.rutgers.edu/boatramps

Sustainable Seafood

Monterey Bay Aquarium's Seafood Watch:

http://oceana.org/en/living-blue/sustainable-seafood-guide

SeaChoice's sustainable seafood search and ranking:

www.seachoice.org/search

Appendix II: Boat Greening Checklist

- [ ] Wash with water only (use substitutes for harsh chemicals).

- [ ] Apply good wax on the hull.

- [ ] Use the least harmful antifouling materials.

- [ ] Use and maintain the pumps and holding tank for black and, potentially, gray water.

- [ ] Use a sewage pump-out facility whenever available.

- [ ] Maintain your engine and watch for leaks.

- [ ] Do not pump bilge water directly into the water (unless it is only water).

- [ ] Read labels of the products you use; look for the EcoLogo in Canada. In the US, look for Green Seal or DfE but be aware that you should always read labels to find out ingredients.

- [ ] Don't use biologically harmful chemicals such as phosphates, ammonia, chlorine, caustic soda, surfactants, or potassium hydroxide near the water.

- [ ] Take precautions to avoid spreading exotic species.

- [ ] Practice proper refueling procedures.

- ❏ Repackage, reuse, and recycle everything that you can.

- ❏ Take garbage and recyclables to shore for proper disposal.

- ❏ Be careful what you do onshore too; much water pollution originates on land.

- ❏ Help to dispose of derelicts in your area.

- ❏ Help your marina to adopt green practices and share your knowledge with fellow boaters.

- ❏ Report suspected violations of boating laws promptly.

- ❏ Keep your distance from marine mammals and report those that come too close.

- ❏ Keep up-to-date on green boating practices by reading publications and websites listed in Appendix I.

- ❏ Report violations, or environmental hazards, or disasters to the appropriate authorities so they can be dealt with promptly.

OTHER TITLES OF INTEREST FROM SELF-COUNSEL PRESS

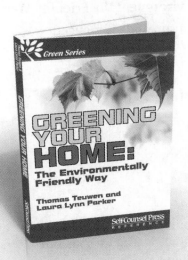

Greening Your Home:
The Environmentally Friendly Way

Thomas Teuwen & Laura Lynn Parker
ISBN 978-1-77040-207-2
6 x 9 • paper • 128 pp.
First Edition: October 2014
$12.95 USD/CAD

We all want a more environmentally smart home, but many of us worry it will cost too much, be too difficult to fix or maintain, and not worth the bother. Not so. This book identifies the practical path to a more sustainable household, from how we can save energy to how we can keep clean to how we can intelligently use and reuse in an affordable, easy way. Good environmental practices need not be intimidating or expensive. This book, part of the Self-Counsel *Green* series, shows you the way.

The Authors

Thomas Teuwen spent 25 years starting, owning, and managing three small companies in the manufacturing, mining, energy, and technology sectors. He also served as a founding member on the board of the Offshore Trade Association of Nova Scotia, as president of the Cape Breton Offshore Trade Association, as Executive Director of Vision: Community Initiatives for Regional Development, and as cochair of the remediation subcommittee of the Sydney Tar Ponds Project.

Laura Lynn Parker began her professional career as a Residential Counsellor, furthered her education in the United States, then moved backed to Canada as an Audiologist. She left the field after a decade to move into the field of web design and writing.

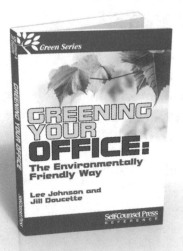

Greening Your Office:
The Environmentally Friendly Way

Lee Johnson and Jill Doucette
ISBN 978-1-77040-208-9
6 x 9 • paper • 128 pp.
First Edition: October 2014
$12.95 USD/CAD

Your office is your home away from home, and we all want it to be environmentally friendly and safe. But it's usually someone else's job. This book, part of the Self-Counsel *Green* series, helps your office find more sustainable practices to save energy, reduce waste, and ultimately save money. It helps you develop a new office culture that leads the way in smart techniques to minimize your environmental footprint and build a stronger sense of your team's purpose.

The Author

Lee Johnson is the Program Manager of the Vancouver Island Green Business Certification Program which is run under the not-for-profit Synergy Sustainability Institute. The program was built to recognize the efforts of local businesses that are reducing their environmental impact. For businesses, it is a guide to greening their operations and educating staff. For consumers, it is a symbol that lets them know which businesses have green practices.

Jill Doucette dreams big and makes it happen. A small-town girl from the interior mountains of BC, she has quickly become one of the green gurus of the West Coast. Active in many local non-profits and businesses, Jill's fuel is innovation, which constantly puts her creative juices into overload turning virtually any problem into a solution. Jill is passionate about building a green economy in BC where local business and ecology can thrive.

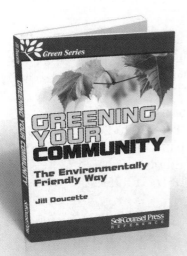

**Greening Your Community:
The Environmentally Friendly Way**

Jill Doucette
ISBN 978-1-77040-223-2
6 x 9 • paper • 128 pp.
First Edition: October 2014
$12.95 USD/CAD

Throwing a block party? Creating a community garden? Building a playground? Helping an ailing neighbor with a food circle? Jill Doucette, founder of Synergy which works to catalyze the green economy, helps you strengthen your community with sustainable ideas to environmentally improve where you live.

The Author

Jill Doucette dreams big and makes it happen. A small-town girl from the interior mountains of BC, she has quickly become one of the green gurus of the West Coast. Active in many local non-profits and businesses, Jill's fuel is innovation, which constantly puts her creative juices into overload turning virtually any problem into a solution. Jill is passionate about building a green economy in BC where local business and ecology can thrive.

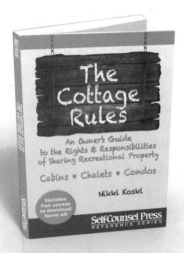

**The Cottage Rules:
An Owner's Guide to the Rights &
Responsibilites of Sharing
Recreational Property**

Nikki Koski
ISBN 978-1-77040-200-3
6 x 9 • paper + download kit • 112 pp.
Second Edition
$12.95 USD/$13.95 CAD

The Cottage Rules sets out no-nonsense, easy-to-use guidelines for cottage owners who share ownership with others. It deals with everything from succession to laundry. The rules work to prevent conflicts, so that your relationship with your partners can be either as close or as distant as you desire. This book shows cottage owners how to manage their cottage like a business, which in turn prevents disputes and frees time and energy so they can use it to enjoy the cottage. With four cornerstones to the system (meetings, bookings, banking, and work weekends), the rules are easy to implement, flexible, and reliable. *The Cottage Rules* can help owners attain their dream of peaceful cottage ownership. Also included is a set of forms and samples as part of a download kit.

This long overdue second edition is more comprehensive and includes the addition of new chapters.

The Author

The Malette family has owned a cottage for more than 30 years, and it was inherited by Nikki and her siblings from their father. Nikki and her husband Russ created a system to ensure against future conflicts, and Nikki Koski has now written this book to share the system with you. When she is not at the cottage, Nikki Koski works as a real estate agent.

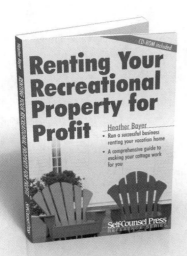

Renting Your Recreational Property for Profit

Heather Bayer
ISBN 978-1-55180-733-1
6 x 9 • paper + CD-ROM • 176 pp.
Second Edition
$15.95 USD/$19.95 CAD

Renting Your Recreational Property for Profit is the definitive guide to the cottage rental business. It contains everything the cottage owner needs to know to rent a cottage professionally and profitably.

Many people begin renting out their recreational property without first researching the business. This book provides the background knowledge and additional tips they will need to make it a success.

The Author

Heather Bayer is CEO of CottageLINK Rental Management, a leading cottage rental agency based in Ontario, Canada, and director of Clearwater Holidays, a UK tour operator that promotes cottage vacation rentals in Canada to the British and European markets. Bayer writes articles and delivers seminars on all aspects of recreational property purchase and vacation rentals.